austerity

RADIATOR PRESS
Philadelphia, PA. USA

Printed & Bound in the USA
First Edition
ISBN 978-1-7328145-1-6

Artwork on cover by Nicole Donnelly "Processes of Loss," 2017
Design by Kim Gek Lin Short
Macho and Mrs. Eaves
www.radiatorpress.com

Marion Bell
austerity

Radiator Press

1 OH DON'T
3 Five Years

5 AUSTERITY I
23 AUSTERITY II
59 DEVOTION
73 GAY GROUP

OH DON'T

don't valorize
oh don't
valorize
strength
which hasn't
actually
brought you
here

Five Years

"The last few years I have been evolving and becoming more real, more intimate and more human."

"The world today is a very different place than the one we lived in back in 2010. 2010 seems like ancient history now."

— Chelsea Manning from "moving on"

I was someone else five years ago & I realize I was changing with everyone else when I thought I was on my own. we think about your courage while doing other things. while not feeling brave enough.

AUSTERITY I

Knowing about someone's struggle and seeing them exist anyway and sometimes that's how I feel about you.

— Mattilda Bernstein Sycamore

AUSTERITY

Look i get radicalized by love
like any normal
American

i wouldn't turn you into a wife
i'm a person you know
and the conditions are weird
the naiveté
even of my knowing
i wouldn't turn you into anything

i get radicalized by love
and by austerity
and by work
by austerity and by work

it's easy to get radicalized just by paying
        attention to experience
i would write to you
in the naiveté of my knowing

june 18th 2013

It's 3 in the morning & I've just spent all night alone on the internet. It's the end of June? time feels tremendously strange. It's 3 in the morning and I just looked at david wojnarowicz's scanned diary pages – pictures of his journals on the internet and then I could write something out of the intense, submerged feeling I live in – which is something about the closeness of anxiety, yearning and actual love, actual love and recognition which I do feel a great deal of but am held back from approaching, speaking to –

I'm trying to work out
my object relations

the small self made books of
women who write poetry

who i fall in love with
again & again

I say to Ben and to Leah

"I wish we could recognize what people needed us to recognize"

JULY

jigsaw
circle

riding the trolley
and returning

july erupting

a heaven of grief

trying to mean the acts
of humility

i'm not performing right now

he said

the streets being
canyons of heavy light
seeing the same faces

on the trolley

and

every demonstration in the heat

the recognition of
strangers
becomes very precious

a mantle
a mantilla
a heavy thing to carry

to make love in this sadness
or this heat

i'm repeating my standards of care
i'm repeating the standard of care

to feel feelings in public
with strangers
is
becoming
the most important thing

TROUBLE

someone who's
in trouble
sometimes
if i make
my trouble an
intellectual thing
then i can sit at the table
sometimes

w
i
n
t
e
r
/
2
0
1
4

the lucidity of
my bedroom when
i wrote poems a
million years ago
all the lights were
on

because i was raised by literature and literature
was invented to sing
about lost love

well for those and the other reasons
i don't forget

you can't enter the struggle
as an object
\in the place of the million things
why that/

i love you/ i try not
to be cruel to myself
anymore

my hand is unsteady
my handwriting

i don't know what poetry is
or why i'm loyal to it
(if) i want clarity
if i can pursue a difficult
honesty that way

the thoughts i have

if only if only
people's illness could be respected
like people's strength and goodness
actual and particular

DREAM - December 1st, 2014

I've made a movie or I'm doing a performance – I'm in a restaurant – I'm doing a performance about my love – my unrequited love for the woman who works in the restau-rant – we have had a love affair that has not been fulfilled – the woman is watching and an audience is also watching – the performance is very moving – it is a success - I leave the restaurant and I am paying the woman I have loved but not well – I am paying her for a meal – our love has not been a success but the performance has been – there is an over-whelming feeling of recognition between us – she gives my money back to me after I pay – she pushes it back to me + I say no no and I give it back to her

summer 2014

you two are
thick as thieves

Say the word "reparation"

Try
Try

Take B6 to remember your dreams

What's scary about those things
you've already had
in droves

what's so scary about what
you've already
lived thru?

"what middleclass
person doesn't wear
class drag"

"everybody wants to be

elite and
a man of the people"
what we turn against
the other coast
what we move against
"the room in candlelight"

i may be old-fashioned
about the repressive hypothesis
but it almost killed me

if community is everyone you
meet
and i do and don't

you're being really
polite
considering what
you went through
is one's resistance more than
contrariness
(yes)

what is a speech act?
what is closeness?

who am i now?
"it's a square party that needs to be crashed"
look at the medicine
it's only friendship
people's good deeds

a shift in representation
without a shift in conditions
or to speak of representation
without speaking of the conditions of production

sense of the inexplicable lifted away
the sense
lifted away
don't make me describe
a workday

inside jokes
on the queer kids
we're not
kids
anymore
your body takes a stance
when you speak
in friendship

"it is so lovely"
it is so
lovely
the briefness
and

you gotta stop saying neoliberal
everybody wants to resist it

"weepy white lady feminism"
everybody wants to resist it
by being an asshole in their own
special way

the sweetness of experience
implicates nostalgia
for the beauty of the past
which you only barely survived
try to touch it with a dramatic phrase
to walk with friends
on the streets
in july

moments you wish you had precise and detailed journal
entries about, the loveliness and complexity of- but in the

moment you were sloppy worried pressured by other things-
forgettable things which also fill the days

if i'm wrong about the repressive hypothesis
whatever
you're medicine
your medicine
identification outside or across
ok
keep moving
deeply moving
feeling is a kind of movement
be ready be ready

where do i go now in the love which is writing
in the writing which is love
like a fan spreading
the form of a person
dark dark
the materiality of friendship
i cry for
the darkness a person lives
in
seeing

the dark side of you/

the dark side of me

disavow disavow

the dark side of you and the dark side of me

when you think of a person

I don't want to be on their "bad side"

don't ever cross them

to cross from one side to the other

"you have to put your money where your mouth is all the time

or else it just sounds like east coast liberalism 2014"

the spiritual quality that allows you

to   move

through

if they thought your

performance

wasn't legible

well fuck them
our experience
isn't even legible
to ourselves
sometimes
even when we
work in the dark
trying

AUSTERITY II

"The image of character as stamped or branded by its early experience of shame captures a sense of the indelible nature of ideology's effects."

— Heather Love

"But aren't we born of her? Didn't we queer her body being born?"

— Hilton Als

"The most important point of view for all of us is, I believe in this example, only Brutus can kill us. Only the person who can't kill us can kill us."

— Hélène Cixous

"...but you realize that I'm like the other lesbians, willing to become the political nurse for anyone I meet."

— Paul B. Preciado

the Philadelphia police department puts a flyer in our mailbox suggesting we find them on various social media platforms

* * *

the tv anchors
make a point of telling us they feel the tear gas
"it stings, Rachel"

when something big is happening and you
can only be aware of tiny
things your body is doing
that my pants are too tight
and there's a big pimple on my chin

how do you know each other?

the border cop asks

try to keep the space of
travel for a minute the aura of it
an inner life
like to aspire to what is already there
all my life
I've been dreaming of an inner life
in which I'm also standing on
the street

google ocd about....

and up pops the most compelling searches

ocd about cleaning

ocd about hiv

ocd about being gay

ocd about time

austerity

a dance party up front
and a fire in the backyard
at the new queer punk house
on 51st street
all the quiet girls
sitting together around the fire

another bookstore philosophy section with no women

As if speaking to a person more quiet than myself

I can beat you at your own game. Like we would defeat our exes by making better art than them. As if that would approach reparation for the years I was young and cute and living in violence.

my temporal drag is a black trucker hat black sweatshirt

My poem fails when the I that is the I of the poem or the I of my life fails to relate.

What depends on timing   that which depends on timing
jokes, music, poetry, love

Who slays me and who gives me life. I need both of these. I need all of it.

(The poem is saved by an address.)

on the 51st street walking bridge

over railroad tracks

graffiti in pink

says

STOP BLAMING YOURSELF

STOP BLAMING YOUR FRIENDS

the waif you were and

are

modest handsome/

people who've shown up in my life/at

the end of winter

Again against my own perverse and obsessive loyalty
If I put too much pressure on myself to be liberated and
    then I put too much pressure on myself to be disciplined
I wonder what disciplines my body waking up early to work
even though I'm sick

    As if a person liberates their own body.

If I've tried so hard to make my poetry embarrassing excessive gay in all the ways I've not been in my life. Well that can only take me so far. If community is everyone you meet. The way people I'm too nervous to talk to become huge influences on my thought.

Later maybe try to trust my own perverse and obsessive loyalty which has also led me astray or put me in the wrong place.

They said the way not to feel alienated is to have a few close friends. She said how many times do you think we've kissed. It would never occur to me to think in math like that. But thousands. Five thousand. Ten thousand.

Austerity is a series of measures the point of which I forget. I just know the tenor of it. Cutting everybody's food stamps and going to war. Again. Forever. A liberation movement that crests and falls. Falls for thirty years.

An explicitness which exceeds itself. Needs itself. I'm a dropout and it's so comforting. To spend your days off reading enormous books and not going out.

That too, only takes you so far.

This desire for emotional explicitness. Like I listen to confessional singers more than I read experimental poetry. The desire fulfills itself. Beyond us. In Jim's high-rise apartment I pull out his old Tim Dlugos books. They were out of print by the time I loved his poetry. But Jim knew him. He was there.

In the new park they've built in front of city hall — what was wreckage for the last few years after the occupy encampments were destroyed now a plaza full of people. How long ago was that fall and spring? This space is open again after years of being fenced and full of ruins,

When I was so wild and used to dream of discipline. And now all I can do is ask what are the forces that discipline my body – all I can do is ask, knowing what they are. Knowing all the names.

Brandon writes Marx in the morning, Benjamin at night. We used to work together and our nicknames were Rough Trade and Butchie. Our nicknames for ourselves. That winter we were the saddest baristas on the whole coast. At work one day Brandon showed me a tarot card that made things possible again. It was the smallest nuance. The most subtle opening. In a hallway, in a day full of snow.

Leah showed up that spring. The spring after the saddest winter.
She showed up at a job I got fired from.
She appeared there out of nowhere.
(At the big gay doctor's office)
a harbinger
I guess
of the nurses we would be
to each other.

What I write to myself

on a sunday

waiting to be saved

by an

address

"the fragmented also have a right

to subjectivity"

If you realize and you always realize in time that may be years too late. It's easy to say queer time. That helps a lot to say. To describe it that way. That you've undone yourself in your willingness. To be a political nurse. To everyone you meet.

I touch your thigh under the table where I am surrounded by friends drinking wine. I reach under the table to reassure you or reassure myself. Your leg which is so solid covered in layers for winter. I am touching you while surrounded by friends and this is very very lovely.

As if a person liberates their own body
waiting as if to do
undo
the willingness
you call loyalty
perversely
we start
i use your names
in another place
come back
forget
the talk
of austerity
around the table
we forget
the talk
of austerity
i use your names
waiting

* * * * * * * * *

Forgive me these fragments
the connections I begin
to make
but that are elided
I think I started to write narrative poetry - here
the story of love
which stutters
& is material
that happens also
while looking for work
so you can keep living
to undo
what work does
help me continue the story
that is interruption
love that is interruption

DEVOTION

we have willed

difficult
lives

which doesn't make
us

brave

MOST OF THE TIME/REALISM

I'm sitting on the couch while cooking
rice and beans
dreaming again   I guess
            of delivery from realism
the curse of doing the
stupidest jobs
in a soulful way
that's a curse yes
when you said
my new poems were
quiet
I didn't feel good about it
but I'm trying to draw a line
between email you and
the you that is my friend
the you of the poem
and the you that is
my friend
years ago
when we all became friends
while drinking too much
at poetry readings

it makes me feel better when
somebody on tumblr says nostalgia
might be queer hope
it makes me feel more hopeful about
my nostalgia
the curse of always
having the wrong job
of meeting you when
you were straight
bad timing
which is also a
way of being
hopeful
in another world
I said
I feel so
stupid
which was a way
of saying the world
had put me
in the position to
feel that way

you can make
a life
out of shitty jobs
that leave you weird
kinds of time
you can make a life
that way
too
maybe
I use Marxist
language
in team meetings
the use of the word
team at work still
captures
me emotionally
like a socialist dream in
a capitalist context
you're still sleeping upstairs
from working the night shift
and I get mad at you
for missing me

for more
capitalist
bad timing
for more work
but maybe I can end this
by addressing
you sleeping
upstairs
who understands
the jokes
I rely on too much
the joke is that the other
world
can't read us
it's not funny at all
but you know what
I mean
most of the
time

"if our"

if our genitals
aren't symmetrical
we'll make other
kinds
of symmetry
anal and
clitoral
together
at the same time
that i've
          changed to
mirror you if
mirroring is
          what you need
          sometimes
that i have this too large dick
that i wear this
big dick
not even knowing
if i want to
just because someone
has to

save me from realism

save me from my documentary

don't save me from my desire

if we say the

double bind

it won't dissolve

if i go through these

abjections

i find

meaningful so i can keep

living

double bind

i read these volumes of civil rights history

all summer

weeping whenever people

behave with

courage

am i being
sentimental
or spiritual?
trying to spit
out the worst

i watch you change
the most beautiful

in another lifetime you said
there's no shame in failing

if i've repressed my
spirituality
because it repressed me
once
a million years ago
and forever
i'm exhausted
from repression

nic bravo says on twitter
normo lezzies
sound like dudes

because they don't have a mode
of desiring women
that isn't patriarchal
i read this to my girlfriend
in bed
i think this is very profound
it hurts

my sexuality kept
getting mistaken
for butch competence

the double bind
anal and
clitoral
distant symmetry
i called to

what's historical time/when we need 20,000 dollars today/what's historical time/what's ten years/in the urgency of now/what's three years/in historical time/baby we're going to die/i'm trying to work for wages from home/ precarious, i guess/munching on snacks/ "remotely"/ we're not going to die/ today/ i'm crying and making no sense/ we haven't been biopolitically/ selected for premature death/ i promise not today / last summer/ the summer before / if it's ten years before the institutions will agree that we are valid today

running on
devotion
and
antidepressants
i read
George Jackson's
prison letters
on the 124
bus
where the
working classes
ride far away from the city
for low wage
jobs
learning to think differently
this tremendous
exhaustion
which is actually my body
saying i don't give a fuck
about money or
poetry
i don't care about anything
but being here for you
now

GAY GROUP

gay group therapy

it's a feeling in a room with boundaries

the feeling is liminal and collective

to be angry on behalf of someone else

it was a weird inbetween feeling to carry

I waited to feel embarrassed but it didn't come

the other

language
in the other
time
languages i don't/
speak
why one is nostalgic
even unto
for suffering
but that was
life
it was life
and that is one's
own life that
won't happen again
+ remains
insoluble
really

lately i devolve
or come to simply
take naps
it's still February
 i get so nostalgic
in my writing for younger me

i felt yearning even
for when my bed was a mattress on the
floor- tucked behind
the bookshelf in the
corner on hazzard st

psychic worry
is like thinking
but i'm worried about
"my writing"
like it doesn't need to be good
but i need to need it
that she was lucky that
she was lucky to have me
this was surprising
but made me
feel very warm

last night there was
a moment
i wanted to record and transcribe
her words into a poem bc
they were so astonishing
she kept talking & i felt almost
less real because i don't talk very much
but i'm not less real

gay people are too nice
Jackie kept saying

DON'T BE TOO NICE
stop being nice
stop being too nice

when i am with 2 queer people i feel
safe
i feel like i am a woman but also not
that at all

what she was saying was
something about how real her ass was
the realest
the most real

I think being gay
is believing in friendship
and feeling nostalgic
for sadness

like being a 22 year old bar dyke

in the bar that doesn't exist anymore

LITERATURE FOR NON-LITERARY ENDS

to push against the container

to insert what is “too much”

to do bad writing

Space heater/
&

overhead lamps

neil young

always

stupid ambient

streetscape

not knowing then
about the persistence of certain kinds
of ambivalent memory

ambivalence
the cobbled street

no I dont mean no I don't mean

typing typing

here's a pocket of memory

I transferred from one computer to another

a million selfies before they were even called that
beauty when it didn't mean
that
the autonomy
damaged autonomy
of my apartment on Susquehanna avenue
where I did so much typing

it's a pocket that the words only move around

but I dreamed of taking someone I loved

back to that apartment
I dreamt of it
last night
the first night of
2016

we're all so alive
writing to each

other inscribed

I think so

you're a tree   cutnpaste   trees growing into each
other uhuh   trees growing into each   our anxieties
inflect each other   I think I got a new anxiety disorder
when I fell in love w you

"Why is it that things an instance before they have happened already seem to have happened?" — Clarice Lispector

"And trauma is always like this, it creates a vacuum, a loss of memory, a silence from which we must move forward."
— AA Bronson

not to write or be enough in the moment (dear   dear   dear) the long moment before or after another rupture we survive suddenly without memory   if i could have written in certain nests of speech with you to remember what we said   you're my hero you texted me in the long before a rainy September morning i archive forever   i took pictures of my face there   was nothing else to do to rediscover something you lived – you loved/ rather / you don't have to pay me / you're fam / friendship and love / a slippage between / addressed / is always a luminous category / I never quite fit / but am awed by / thank you for letting me borrow your car / to take a long drive and listen to sad songs / thank you for helping me move / you don't have to buy me a beer / I'm less precarious than you right now

moving away from the ocean   fall out   ash monster
of grieving   map in the head map in the head of back
street   cul de sac   small block   alley
lists we made   against our
an interruption you   treat
as music as music   as movement
you never had a trajectory
what is an alwaysness
looking at the house from the outside
think about attenuation of pronouns   we we they they
amethyst   rock
I'm sorry   imminent rain of February
they lived together in a rowhouse for how long 20 years
both of his lovers died in the same year   and he kept living
you keep those facts like if you wore a rose
quartz necklace which you don't

committed to what can only be approached by trust which is impossible to imagine after the things we've lived thru/ still it's the approach / it's the only address/ what keeps us addressable/ the real future is the otherness we can't imagine/ and even I can't defeat that in myself/ it's so resilient because it's beyond me

December Journal/2017

secret idea
of yours
that you
could become a better person
if you read the right books

at the ica fred moten speaks of "battling with identity against the backdrop of the denial of identity"

yes yes yes

I have to fight against my urge to ascetism and self-sacrifice
but I'm reading about simone weil again -- she seems like the most beautiful
she says, "when you decide something always do what will cost you the most"

I would like there not to be grants
no crowdfunding
no paperwork to prove your need
no application to decide who gets to live

I create the conditions for my heartbreak or a neoliberal self-help book wants me to think so

the word for spirit
the need to document
as a way of being
"attending to"

friend notes

Ben writes to me, *queer and trans people aren't good at supporting each other despite the rhetoric. Facebook likes aren't support, Instagram hearts aren't either.*

I write to Ben that I feel like we need to do a lot of research – a lot of background research to understand the context of each person in our lives.

Reading lists
of what people
need to
understand us

"I'm sure/ you can see me better / than I can. / Dealing with one-sided particulars, loneliness, contempt and godliness."
— Mike Cavuto actually texts me these lines from Kyger

Acknowledgments

This book is for Leah Basarab – my best friend – this weird writing comes out of grief and empathy we've moved through together. You always make me braver.

Thank you to all the poets in Philly, named and un-named, who have changed my life.

Jim Cory for endless generosity, grace, wit and support.

Mike Cavuto for believing in my poems, for faith and vision.

Ryan Eckes and Ian Davisson, it means everything to me that the two of you are publishing this.

Love to the people who make life worth living and writing about: Ben Singer, Jackie Caselle, Jesse, Marisa Kling, Andi Grushka, Brandon Holmquest, Gabey Conver.

Nicole Donnelly, I am so grateful to be able to use your sculpture as a cover image and for all the long processes in your work.

Also, thank you to the Barbara Deming Foundation and the Leeway Foundation for supporting my work.

MARION BELL is a poet, social work student and mental health worker living in Philadelphia. She has been shaped by Philly poetry communities over the last decade.

www.radiatorpress.com